I Want to Love Life: A Collection of LGBT Themed Poetry

Cris Black

BookLeaf Publishing

India | USA | UK

Presentation by *BookLeaf Publishing*

Web: www.bookleafpub.com

E-mail: info@bookleafpub.com

ISBN: 9789360944919

First edition 2024

Welcome

I am invited, some would say often
But I never feel welcome

You smile and hug to say hi, and talk like you've
known me a lifetime
And maybe it's just me who feels this way

You joke and laugh, and I laugh too, but I can't
stop thinking about home

Home is where I feel welcome
Because I have my room, I have my life all
wrapped up with all the things I like to do

Or liked to do
But I find myself not feeling welcome there, too

I am often invited there, and now don't feel
welcome anywhere.

The Black Sheep

When you are the black sheep you hide a lot of
yourself.

You do talk about yourself, but only some parts
because if you say the full thing you will be
further of an outcast

No one knows the full you because no one will
understand

You finally tell people like you and you can
finally be you,
and then they go away and you are back to being
trapped.

You finally start sharing with others
and they think you are crazy for what you
believe, for what you are

For me, I am
Queer
Non-binary
And more

Secret

I have a secret, something I hold onto strongly
and only share with some.

I don't share it with everyone because I know
not everyone will like it; not everyone will
understand it; not everyone will respect it.

Not everyone will respect me, my identity.

It took me a long time to figure it out
completely, to accept it, to live by it.
Now that I have, I don't want to hide it but I
have to.

There are some crowds that knows about it,
there are some who respect it, there are some
who understand it, and there are some who also
live by it
but that is not everyone, and I know I cannot
fully live by it
and be open about myself to every single person.

And it sucks, it really does, because even with
knowing all this general information, it hurts
even more that you are a part of it too.

It doesn't hurt that you don't understand, I know it's hard sometimes, but it hurts that you don't respect it and you immediately deny it every single time.

This is not your identity, it's mine.

Boxes

We live in a world where people love boxes -
they love putting everyone in them

But we cannot make new boxes when none fit us
because some people are open to those boxes,
but most are not

In a world where people love boxes, they only
love certain ones;
the ones that work for them and that they respect

When someone cannot fit into one box, they are
an outcast -
they should not be spoken to, at least not more
than a "hello"
if they even get that, and should not be respected

In a world where that is changing and becoming
more open, not everyone listens or respects it,
respects people.
Not everyone even tries.

Letting Go

Sometimes you just have to let go of what could
be because what is reality is different, and won't
change

You can get stuck on the dreams, the positive
"what if's", to where you don't see the cycle of
negatives you have been through, and will
continue to go through

They can say they will change, but in reality
they don't. They can talk forever about changing
but I see no change, no attempt, just more of the
same

I have been through this, many times before, and
I have done
everything I can to make it work, look past what
people have said and done

I have given them the time and space to change
and they don't, they won't

But one day you wake up and realize you just
have to let go

You have to let go of the dream, let go of the
hope, let go of all the time and energy spent
trying to make it work

You have to let go of the positive memories,
because they aren't coming back. They won't be
like that anymore.
Sometimes you just have to let go of what could
be because what is reality is different, and won't
change

You can get stuck on the dreams, the positive
"what if's", to where you don't see the cycle of
negatives you have been through, and will
continue to go through

They can say they will change, but in reality
they don't. They can talk forever about changing
but I see no change, no attempt, just more of the
same

I have been through this, many times before, and
I have done
everything I can to make it work, look past what
people have said and done

I have given them the time and space to change
and they don't, they won't

But one day you wake up and realize you just
have to let go

You have to let go of the dream, let go of the
hope, let go of all the time and energy spent
trying to make it work

You have to let go of the positive memories,
because they aren't coming back. They won't be
like that anymore.

Too Much

Some things just take too much energy

When you fight with everyone around you
for being who you are

I don't understand how people fight everyone
who doesn't acknowledge them

I understand the pain, the want to be respected

But I don't understand why the need to correct
When you will never see them again
Or when it's clear they don't care and never will

When none of it changes who you are
I don't understand the constant fight
And not to just live

A Fresh Start

Are you ready to leave all you thought behind,
all you have behind, for a fresh start?

The memories, the feelings, the friends

Lies - how they can spread and trap you but also
help you learn and move on

The pain of what you could have had even if its
not real
but why fixate on something that's fake?

Familiarity - its safe and comforting but it's a
trap that can drag you so far down

A trap - you can fall into one at any time and
with anyone
and not even know it
but when you figure it out and are free there is
nothing holding you back

A fresh start - I am ready to grow and be free,
finally

My Body Is Not My Own

I can look in the mirror and see it, moving as I
do
I can move my finger on an arm, or leg, or
stomach and feel the skin
And yet my body is not my own

I can sit, walk, run, jump and I know my body is
performing those actions
I can eat and sleep and breathe and know it is for
my body to be healthy
And yet my body is not my own

Someone else can hold me and I can feel their
gentle embrace
My partner can make love to me and I know it is
my body in the act
And yet my body is not my own

I think of myself and how I look
and it is not what appears in front of that mirror,
or performing those actions,
or making love to my partner

It is not what I look like
It is not who I am

Dysphoria

It's not that I don't believe you
when you tell me I'm beautiful

It's that this face and body is not mine
Not the one I see when I close my eyes

It's not that I don't appreciate the compliment
But sometimes it's too much when my skin is
crawling

Heartbeat

It starts with my heartbeat, of the pace and
intensity increasing
My breathing increasing like I just ran up flights
of stairs.

Acutely aware of everything about me,
Everything I want gone, everything that doesn't
fit.

My chest tightening, tingling as if trying to
disappear.

My back and shoulders is where it goes next,
tingling like static on a screen
but being so uncomfortable its to the point of
pain.

My head spinning, panicking, then dissociating

I am left with but a shell of who I am because of
what I was perceived to be.

Shell

I am a shell of a person

I do everything as I should
But yet I don't feel, not fully

I think so many pieces of me has died
That I can never fully be a whole person againI
am a shell of a person

I do everything as I should
But yet I don't feel, not fully

I think so many pieces of me has died
That I can never fully be a whole person again

Head

I have so much going on in my head all the time
that I thought I felt nothing
When in reality, I feel everything with such
intensity that it overwhelms me.

I Want to Love Life

I want to hear birds chirping
I want to feel the waves under my hands
I want to see tree blowing in the wind
and smile.

I want to talk to people
and make meaningful connections
and laugh, alongside others.

I want to dance in the rain
and sing in the shower
and love life.

I want to love the good parts about life,
but I also want to love the bad too
because even in the bad there is good
and you cannot truly love life without loving it
all.

So I want to love the sadness
I want to love the heartbreak
because I want to love the lessons

I want to love the struggle
I want to love the pain

because I want to love the strength.

I want to love the loss
I want to love the confusion
because I want to love the growth.

I want to love the good parts about life,
but I also want to love the bad too
because even in the bad there is good
and you cannot truly love life without loving it
all.

Untitled

There are a million different ways it could end
badly

But there's one path where it won't
and you cannot let the possibility of something
bad happening ruin it

Happiness

I can find happiness, moments or situations
which sparks pure joy and even glee sometimes

But I will never truly be happy without changing
everything.

Trust

I don't know if I'd ever be able to fully trust
again

From countless broken promises
to betrayal by friends, family, and partners

I've been fed lies, with no way of knowing the
truth
I've been told secrets, that turned out not to be
true

There's the story of one with no match from the
other
And the truth I can never see

Now you can open up and talk to me
and I won't be able to believe you
Because of all the countless lies told to me

Devastation

It can hit at any second and turn your whole life
upside down

It doesnt care if you were having the best or
worst day before it

It finds pleasure in seeing your brain start
spinning, your heart start racing, your not being
able to catch your breath and feeling like you are
about to faint

The thing you dread most happening, or even
something you don't even expect, can and will
happen.

Death

"Why are you so scared of me?" Death asked
"Because you mean the ending of so many more
experiences I could have" I answered.

Door

I talked to Death
He was standing by a door,
Telling me everything would be ok.

I move closer, pain subsiding
feeling lighter with every step

The pain I felt, so long now
"Everything will be ok."

We talked for a while, though only minutes
passed. About life, and death, and decisions.

"I can't go through," I told him
I must go back.

"Then quickly now, as there isn't much time
left"

Feeling peace right in front of Deaths door, I
turned and ran back. This part of my story isn't
over yet.

Change

Change is different –
difficult even.
It's scary and saddening
to think about a routine
being ruined.
To be so used to something
and it disappears
but you have to change.

Igne natura rebicatur integra

Igne natura rebicatur integra -
Through fire, nature is reborn whole.

You have to experience the worst
before you can experience the best.

You have to know sadness
before you can understand
happiness.

www.ingramcontent.com/pod-product-compliance
Lightning Source LLC
LaVergne TN
LVHW041300200726
843507LV00014B/3073